# Bears

# BEARS

Art, Legend, History

Giorgio Coppin

Series editor: Giorgio Coppin

The Bulfinch Library of Collectibles

A Bulfinch Press Book
Little, Brown and Company
Boston · Toronto · London

First North American Edition

English translation by John Gilbert
Series editor: Giorgio Coppin

**Library of Congress Cataloging-in-Publication Data**

Coppin, Giorgio.
   [Orso. English]
   Bears: art, legend, history/Giorgio Coppin.—1st North American ed.
      p.  cm.  —(The Bulfinch library of collectibles)
   "A Bulfinch Press book."
   ISBN 0-8212-2006-6
   1. Bears—Collectibles.   2. Bears—Legends.   3. Bears—History.
   I. Title. II. Series.
   NK3851.C3613   1993
   704.9'432—dc20                                    92-30866

Bulfinch Press is an imprint and trademark of Little, Brown and Company (Inc.)
Published simultaneously in Canada by Little, Brown & Company (Canada) Limited

PRINTED IN ITALY

# CONTENTS

# Walking flat and reaching high

Of the many characteristics that distinguish the bear – its size, its bulk, its ferocity, even its legendary bad temper – there is probably none that counts for more than its flat-footedness.

Unlike the vast majority of animals, digitigrades who walk on the tips of their feet, either on their toes or on the hooves, the bear is a plantigrade. It supports its entire body weight on the soles of its feet. From this broader base, the bear is able to rear up on its hind legs, adopting an upright stance virtually at will. It can even walk, albeit for short distances, on two legs and will alternate this with its more standard posture on all fours. It is not perfect, of course. With flat feet the bear cannot aspire to the flexibility and grace of such animals as the cat, the dog, the horse or the gazelle. But that does not matter. With feet planted solidly on the ground and its long claws protruding, the bear may be inelegant, but it is content. The posture suits it well. It suited us too. According to most anthropologists, we once carried ourselves in the same way.

The bear's similarity to us, in posture, in physiognomy

6

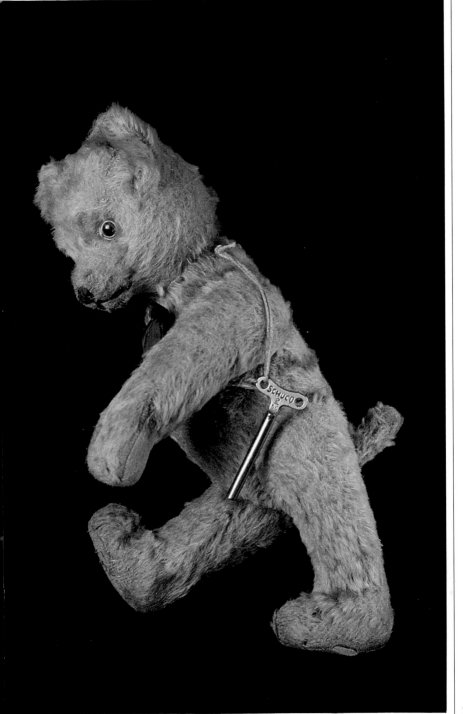

*A metal moneybox from North America,
dated 1896; the coin is balanced on the rifle
of the hunter who shoots it into the bear.*

and in a whole host of other ways, explains much of the animal's position within human societies over the ages. The bear has been feted and worshipped, idolized and adored, virtually since the dawn of history. More recently it has even been adopted as a cuddly children's toy, perhaps the most popular toy in the world. Yet it has also received our wrath: hunted with deadly determination and fought with a degree of ferocity that, even on man's own record, is horrific.

Today the consequences of the persecution are clear. The brown bear which once ranged widely through the woods

*Two bear hunters carrying their prey: they are painted papier-mâché figures for a crib, from around 1910–15.*

and forests of Europe is now threatened with imminent extinction. A few bears still survive in the mountains, but only because they are in protected areas in national parks. For those species that roam the wilder, more remote regions of the world which are relatively untouched by civilization, the situation is brighter. But only just. The Kodiak, the grizzly, the spectacled bear and the polar bear are all in peril.

Today the biggest threat to the bear's existence no longer comes from hunting. It comes from the destruction of the environment, a crime for which humans are no less responsible. Pollution is changing the balance of nature in all of the earth's regions and straining resources to the limit. Its effect upon wildlife in general, and the bear in particular, is catastrophic. It may even be hopeless. And yet, for all the pessimism, one feels that the bear will manage to survive. The bear has always overcome the hardships and hazards of its environment in the past.

Bears live in all climates and environments and have adapted to them well. The brown bear is a survivor par excellence. It is an omnivore which feeds quite happily on any prey it captures: fish, rodents, wild boar, deer, rabbits, worms and insects. Carrion too. But it will also supplement its diet with vegetation: fruit, berries, grass, roots and, of course, honey. The polar bear is no more fussy in its tastes. In the arctic regions that it inhabits it is a formidable hunter and almost exclusively carnivorous. It feeds principally on fresh seal meat but it will not turn its nose up if it comes across a dead whale on its travels. Nor, when the opportunity arises, will the polar bear decline vegetation and roots.

In fact, most bears will eat almost anything they can get hold of and they are equipped to get hold of most things. They are extremely skilled in using their front paws for such tasks as lifting stones to find grubs, digging for insects and roots. Their strong, sharp claws are ideal for scooping holes in the ground and, with the considerable power of the bear's body behind them, they can also be deployed as deadly weapons, capable of killing, with a single blow, prey the size of a wild boar, a deer or a seal.

Bears fish too. All bears can swim and are happy in water. But swimming is also often done for fun. It is as much a way to cool off in hot weather as a means to catch lunch. Climbing trees, throwing branches and walking are also

*With its flat and somewhat oversized feet, this model cardboard bear, fully hinged, stands proudly upright like a soldier. It is part of a set of cardboard animals sold around 1960.*

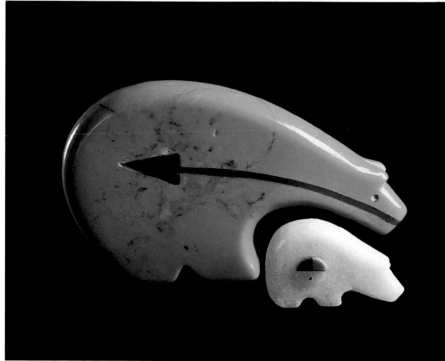

similarly recreational pursuits.

With this in mind, it is easy to see how bears are sometimes regarded as playful fools, splashing about in water and running through woodland. And this image is not completely fanciful. But it is also far away from the truth. Contrary to some impressions, the bear is a creature of considerable resource and high intelligence. It is an excellent hunter and it is no accident that bears have asserted their dominance over almost every other creature in the wild. They have good hearing and a strong sense of smell.

They are born blind. Newborn cubs are helpless and tiny. Their eyes are closed and they cannot walk. Yet they grow quickly on the she-bear's rich fatty milk and within a few months are able to venture away from the den. Bear cubs will, however, remain with their mothers for some time before they are ready to embark confidently on adult life.

In fact, the bear's upbringing is not entirely dissimilar to our own and undoubtedly this resemblance, which also spills over into other attitudes and habits, has had an effect on man's relationship with the animal. It is one of the reasons why we admire bears. But it also explains why we fear the bear, viewing the animal as a rival and an enemy. It is, in a sense, too close for comfort. The bear inspires admiration and fear, affection and hatred in equal measure.

This attitude is by no means a new one. Humankind's conflicting emotions towards the bear stretch back through history and have fostered myths, beliefs and cults all around the world. Rémi Mathieu, a researcher from Paris, is one social scientist who has made this subject a theme of study. In particular he has investigated the place that the bear has occupied in the culture of the ancient Chinese, with its rich store of animal references in tomb frescoes, popular legends and historical texts. What is of greater general interest in

*Two bears from Berne, one drawn on a 1940 postcard, the other photographed in the city's famous Bärengraben or bearpit, sitting on its haunches to show the soles of its feet.*

Mathieu's work, however, is the comparative studies he has made of Chinese and European cultures and those of peoples from Siberia to North America who lack a written literature and thus rely on oral tradition.

Mathieu found that, on both sides of the Pacific, there is an astonishing similarity in the beliefs of those who followed a cult of the bear. Myths, rites, shamanist and magical practices all display an uncanny consonance. Even in diet there are curious duplications. Archaeological finds have indicated that bear flesh was once a fairly common item of food on the menu of past cultures, but as time passed, peoples around the world all came to regard the paws as the only part of the bear's anatomy really worth eating.

In ancient Chinese literature there are references to the habit of eating only the paws, and, more specifically, the palms and soles, of the bear. In Greece, too, both Pliny the

Elder and Plutarch spoke of it as a particular delicacy; and as late as the seventeenth century bears' paws, salted and smoked, were a choice item on the dinner menus of certain German princes.

Bears' paws are flavourful and appetizing, especially when marinated in lemon and oil and then stewed in wine and herbs, but everything points to them having another significance also. Thus there are frequently taboos relating to the method by which the paws may be cooked and, more particularly, how they may be eaten. The paws of the bear were variously forbidden to women, reserved exclusively for them or served to them only after being cooked in a special way. What first appears as a culinary practice is – in origin at least – magical and shamanistic.

The bear's paw has long been attributed with supernatural powers, and not only when eaten. The witch-doctors of the North-West Native American tribes adorned their heads with a crown of grizzly bear claws; the Turks did the same, but using the smaller claws of the brown bear; and shamans from Siberia and Finland fashioned gloves that imitated the paws of bears, complete with claws. This is not to mention the simpler amulets, in their thousands of different forms, which have been worn as ornaments by people of virtually all cultures that had some contact with bears.

In China, two centuries before Christ, Huainan-zu wrote of the prehensile capacity of the bear's paw. In Greece, Aristotle, according to Pliny, noted the resemblance of the animal's hind and front paws to the human foot and hand. It needed only a further small flight of fantasy to assert that the forepaws could grasp objects easily because they consisted of a thumb separated from the other fingers, as with man.

The Native Americans had more savvy, and realized that

*A decorated pottery box designed to contain genuine bear fat. It is English, from around 1880. Until fairly recently, bear fat was used in parts of Europe as an ointment to strengthen babies' limbs.*

*A family group of Teddy bears. They are, in ascending size: a Steiff of 1950, a Schuco dated 1930, a Chad Valley, another Steiff and an Italian model of 1950.*

the secret of the bear's manual dexterity resided in its long claws. But they, too, were sufficiently fascinated by the bear's personality to claim that the analogy with the human hand was not restricted to form and function. One of their legends, for example, tells of a young woman who was tricked one night by the softness of a bear's palm into consenting to marry the beast, convinced that he was a handsome, if somewhat hairy and silent, human youth.

But, while bear paws reign supreme, the value of other parts of the bear's anatomy have not passed altogether unnoticed. The bear is source of a number of medicinal substances: the ancient Chinese used the animal's fat as a remedy for ringworm and falling hair (on its efficacy against the latter, Pliny, too, agreed). In Western Europe, until quite recently, bear fat was still being used, in the form of ointment, for helping delicate babies to stand. And even today, in China, substances from the flesh are extracted as a remedy for rheumatism, from the gall bladder as a medicine for intestinal complaints and from the paws as a tonic.

The bear is also at the root of other all-encompassing beliefs. In primitive cultures, for example, the notion of the bear becoming a superman, or a superman a bear, was widespread and the legends of Greece, Germany, Britain, China and North America abound with heroes who have been so transformed.

Sometimes it was not even a transformation. The bear is often regarded as being a human right from the beginning, albeit an unusual one with an altered appearance. The metamorphosis is thus merely a natural change. This was the conviction of Siberian and North American tribes, to the west and east of the Bering Strait, and of Europeans too, during the Middle Ages. Even today the belief persists in parts of Russia and Poland.

Native Americans regarded the bear as a totemic animal, hence an ancestor. It was addressed as "grandfather" and treated with great respect, even when hunted and killed. Indeed, certain tribes, after killing a bear, would induce it to smoke the pipe of peace to obtain its forgiveness and as a sign of friendship.

The details vary according to the civilization concerned, but the basic belief remains the same: beneath the fur of every bear is, so to speak, a human being trying to get out. The extraordinary consonance of beliefs, myths and legends finds its explanation in this single conviction. Bears and humans have a single origin, a kinship, an immutable link. So strong is this belief rooted that, even today, its residue still persists.

# Bears are beautiful

The largest of all bears, the Kodiak, which lives in Alaska and neighbouring islands, is a massive creature. It is the largest living land carnivore on the planet. It can measure up to 10 feet (3 meters) and weigh almost one ton. The polar bear is a little slimmer, and the grizzly is smaller still and lighter in weight. But even the more modest-sized species, such as the American black bear, are up to twice as heavy as an average man. In addition to its imposing size and weight, the bear also possesses long, sharp, powerful claws and teeth, including massive canines. In overall appearance the animal is not reassuring.

Neither is the bear a social animal. Bears rarely socialize outside their immediate family group and tend to be aggressive to others. They are immediately suspicious of other individuals that approach too close. The female, in particular, when accompanied by her cubs, is extremely fierce and dangerous, permitting neither other bears nor humans to come near her litter.

Confronted by such a fearsome looking creature,

Buon Natale

*The bear is loved as a friend by day and a protector at night. Opposite: a 1910 Christmas card featuring one of the first Steiff Teddies; below: an art nouveau statuette of a sleeping baby cuddling a bear.*

especially when adult, might we not expect to feel awe and dread? We think we should but, in fact, we are more likely to respond with sympathy and even friendship and fellow feeling. It is certainly not by chance that most of the incidents involving bears and humans, some of them fatal, have been caused by our misguided or careless behaviour. Some tourists in North America's National Parks, for example, show the bears ridiculous familiarity and trust, leaving them scraps of food, approaching the animals, or, more foolishly still, attempting to touch and stroke the cubs, paying no heed to the menacing presence of the mother. They treat the bears as if they were entertaining living toys rather than wild beasts that are potentially savage and dangerous.

On the face of it, this is puzzling. Proverbs and sayings warn us against it. When a person is accused of being a

bear we mean surly, grumpy, coarse, selfish and unfriendly – qualities that we all judge to be negative. Most of us, in fact, know very well that the bear is bad tempered, aggressive and hostile. The animal itself is nevertheless seen in a very positive light, its bad points proving no handicap. Why should this be?

Some years ago, Desmond Morris, the distinguished author and student of animal behaviour, described in his book *Manwatching* a research project with 80,000 British schoolchildren between the ages of 4 and 14. They were asked to list their ten favourite and their ten most disliked animals. Among the most popular animals, were the giant panda and the bear, placed fifth and sixth respectively. This was below the chimpanzee, the monkey, the bushbaby (all animals with recognizably human attributes) and the horse, but above the lion, the giraffe and also, perhaps surprisingly, the dog. Among the least popular animals were those that are generally considered dangerous: the snake, the crocodile, the tiger. The lion made it on to both lists, but the bear was absent from the least-liked list. This is a fair reflection of public attitudes as a whole. Bears enjoy a widespread popularity. More, perhaps, than they deserve.

In 1943 the famous Austrian ethologist Konrad Lorenz published a series of findings related to his studies of young birds and mammals. Lorenz showed that these baby animals display certain outward features and certain physical and aesthetic characteristics which evoke, among animals of the same species and often of other species as well, protective rather than aggressive responses. There are, he suggested, a series of infantile characteristics which evoke feelings of parental solicitude and tenderness in adults: the large head in proportion to the trunk; the curved, convex forehead; the massive skull in relation to the face; the large eyes situated

*This little Schuco Teddy bear was made in Germany during the 1930s. The large head, short paws and rounded lines are all childlike features that are inherently appealing, whether in live cubs or toys.*

well below the central line of the face; the short, plump limbs and extremities; the generally rounded shapes; the soft, flexible upper body layers and the round, chubby, prominent cheeks.

Another student of animal behaviour, Danilo Mainardi, extends this list by adding some forms of vocalization and a rather clumsy and uncertain way of moving about. These infantile signals are received favourably by individuals from inside and outside of the same species. "The strong human sensitivity to the infantile signals of other species," writes Mainardi, "is the basis of another evolutionary phenomenon. It is undeniable that the first step towards domestication among many birds and mammals was the blocking of predatory behaviour that such infantile signals generated in their own species, determining an alternative behaviour pattern of adoption."

The bear, even when fully grown, displays many of those infantile features: short, plump extremities; curved, convex forehead; broad, round skull; soft, rounded body parts; soft fur; slow and sometimes rather awkward gait. Looking like an enormous cub, and moreover somewhat like a human (flat feet, upright stance and all), it is little wonder that the creature should stimulate our instinctive, innate protective behaviour. Hence our feelings of tenderness and sympathy, our desire to approach, to touch and even to stroke the animal. We might be interpreting the signals conveyed by its outward appearance wrongly, but it does not matter. They affect us anyway. Indeed, in the case of the bear cub, the signals are so strong as to become virtually irresistible. They release our parental urges almost to the point of actually wanting to adopt the creature.

In 1902 the United States president, Theodore Roosevelt, refused to kill a bear cub, declaring: "If I were to do it I could not look my children in the face." He must

have meant that his children would have disapproved of his actions but, would it be too far-fetched to suggest that Roosevelt was also subconsciously viewing the cub as one of his children too?

# Admiration and fear

The bear is a mythical hero; a courageous and invincible fighter; a sexual rival; a racial ancestor; a near, albeit somewhat wild and hairy, relative; a permanent cub; a father figure; a ferocious beast; a timid, solitary animal; an affectionate and attentive mother who turns violent and dangerous when protecting her young; a circus acrobat; and the best-loved toy in the world.

These various qualities and roles go back in time but their validity is still recognized today. The bear's attributed values have fluctuated, now positive, now negative, but the values themselves remain. In some cases they are blatantly contradictory. Some are firmly rooted in reality, others are free projections of fantasy. Indeed, it is no easy task to detect a common denominator that embraces all the diverse meanings and interpretations that have been attributed to the animal by so many different cultures through the ages. But they still, somehow, make sense. All of them go together to make up what we think of as the bear.

And yet, amidst all these ideas and notions, where do we find the bear itself, the real bear? It hardly exists at all. It has been transformed, instead, into a symbol, an idea, a fantasy.

*Two rather odd-looking bears, seemingly half-real, half-toy (as is evident from their prominent hinges), hold the signboard of a Milanese perfumery on the cover of the 1928 issue of a hairdressers' calendar. This is an early example of the bear's use in advertising.*

The bear is an archetype, a collection of attributed qualities and roles that are deeply rooted in our emotional selves and our subconscious minds. Anthropologists warn us against bestowing human characteristics and qualities on animals, but with the bear it is irresistible.

First of all, it has to be said that the bear is an animal we have taken to our hearts, gladly and freely crediting it with all manner of positive attributes. Our collective memory reserves no special place for animals such as the hyena and the snake, condemned and shunned as unpleasant, repugnant and dangerous. Yet we accept and even welcome the bear, though we know it to be a fierce, aggressive and dangerous creature not to be trifled with. It is undoubtedly an animal to inspire dread, and indeed it has always been

much feared. But there is no other animal with which we so readily identify.

The bear inspires fear, both irrational and justified. But, through identification with the animal and instinctive attraction to it, that fear is in some manner neutralized. It is exorcized because we recognize only the bear's positive values: we see it as a cub that never grows up; as a relative and friend. We admire the determination with which the she-bear nurses, rears and defends her young, and the intelligence of the adult beast in its daily life. The bad points, by contrast, we ignore. In effect, we have created the Teddy bear, the most popular soft toy of all time.

Yet even with the Teddy bear, the ferocity, the strength and the power of the bear have not been entirely

*Three 1930 Steiff Teddy bears pose for an affectionate family snap. The Teddy bear can be seen as the embodiment of all the qualities of an animal cub and of a human baby that characterize a real bear. That is the secret of its appeal.*

neutralized. Rather, it has been transformed and, from being threatening or dangerous, it has become a comfort and source of security.

Beneath the processes of intellect, no matter how noble and sociable, there lies buried in each of us an instinctive subconscious character which inclines towards the primitive and violent, with no gradations or compromises. Hunger, thirst, fear and aggression all bring out primordial instincts that lead us back towards the animal world and reveal the beast in ourselves.

It is difficult and often unpleasant to recognize and accept this bestial part of our nature. But our association with certain animals (with some much more than with others) allows us to put our own instinctive urges in proportion and make light of them. From this point of view, the bear is perfect: bestial yet anthropomorphic, apparently a cuddly toy yet at the same time a strong and protective figure.

So, as the bear is transformed into a toy, into a furry Teddy bear which sublimates all the features of babies and cubs, our doubts and defenses collapse. By a process of identification we transfer to it, without misgiving, the entire baggage of our primitive urges.

Using the bear as a symbol in which we can house our own urges and instincts does not end, however, in the arena of strength and aggression. There are other areas, too, in which the bear's presence provides us with considerable succour and from which the Teddy bear earns its universal and irresistible appeal.

One of the first things a baby instinctively does is touch, stroke and sometimes even yank its mother's hair. This is not surprising. The hair feels soft and comforting and is, in a sense, an extension of the mother's body. But as the baby grows, that comfort inevitably becomes less available. The

*Above: two Viennese bear cubs, in bronze, from the beginning of the twentieth century. Opposite: this engaged couple is also made of bronze, but these bears are Russian and some years older.*

child thus looks for a substitute. So, enter the Teddy bear. Its fur is warm. It moulds itself to the shape of the hand, and the odd strand can even be pulled out without fear of damage or reprimand. Moreover, fur definitely has certain sexual connotations. All in all, because it is covered with soft and sensuous fur, the Teddy bear becomes an irresistibly fascinating toy. The growing child comes to cherish this object, which will often become a constant companion day and night, as tender and loving as the mother herself.

Though at first sight the Teddy bear embodies the conflicting qualities associated with a real bear, in the child's mind it has come to represent something much more personal and intimate. In this process books, stories, films and fairy tales will have all played their part.

Children are powerfully affected by what they read, what they are told and what they see. There is a wealth of literature – stories and comic strips, legends and fables – to enjoy, and a continuous flow of visual entertainment in the cinema and on television. Their experience and conception of animals is moulded at an early age by the animated cartoons of Walt Disney and other film-makers. The bear features prominently in these representations and books and films alike have contrived to transform the image of the real animal into something far more accessible and enticing.

The child envisages the bear as a parental figure, strong but good. It cannot be bad, any more than an all powerful parent can be bad. In the child's imagination, the stronger the bear, the greater its force for good. It does not attack, it defends; it does not threaten, it protects; it is firm but never violent.

Psychoanalysts place great emphasis on the healing process of transference, based on emotions stemming from childhood relationships with parents. They point out that, for every one of us, the first object of transference is a large, powerful animal, resembling our parents. Unlike mother and father, however, who may often be away from home and busy with other things, this substitute animal, the

*A rare example of a 1910 Steiff Teddy bear who is here wearing an embroidered shirt from the same period. Right: a studio portrait of a little girl and her pet Teddy bear, on a 1930 postcard.*

Teddy bear, is always close at hand, always ready to listen, always smiling. We can touch and cuddle it, seeking its protection in the darkness of night. It understands us and judges us.

Children's literature often depicts this mighty creature as being on the lazy side, even rather obtuse – an observation derived, perhaps, from the fact that in nature some bears hibernate or enter a phase of semi-lethargy during winter. But this, too, assists the control mechanisms which enable the child to accept an object which is by definition wild and fierce, without the arousal of disturbing and fearful feelings. Since the animal is inclined to be slow and lazy, the child, who is naturally quick and agile, has no reason to be frightened of it.

Finally, the bear, in its natural surroundings, is associated with a woodland habitat, an environment full of wonder and mystery. The wood is the stage setting, particularly in northern lands, for innumerable myths and legends involving bears. Here the animal can demonstrate to the full its vitality and versatility. The wood is a fascinating amalgam of colours, scents, shapes and sounds, combining to offer a rich source of images to stimulate the creative imagination of story-tellers.

The bear plays an intriguing role in the realm of human imagination, both of child and adult. It is hard to think of any other wild animal that is such a fertile source of inspiration and invention.

# A place in heaven

It is not just in the nursery that the symbol of the bear has prominence. In the heavens too, the bear reigns supreme. It was the Greek philosopher and scientist Thales, living in the seventh to sixth century B.C., who first gave the name "Bear" to the constellations, Ursa Major and Ursa Minor. It just so happens that these are two of the most important constellations in the northern hemisphere. But considering the bear's power in our lives, is it mere accident that Ursa Minor also happens to contain the single most important star in the night sky?

Polaris, the Pole Star, is unique. Shining immobile in the sky in the northern hemisphere it is visible in every season. The other stars circle around it. They play a continual game of hide-and-seek with the horizon, appearing and vanishing during the course of the night. Only Polaris, with the axis of our planet directed straight at it, remains static. The Pole Star is our fixed point in the heavens, the center of an immense wheel of stars.

Thanks to the Pole Star sailors and navigators have been able to find their way across the seas. At dead of night and in

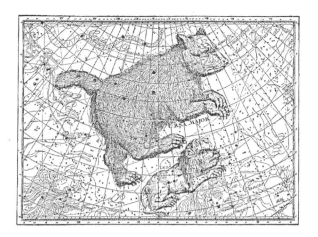

*Ursa Major, the Great Bear, tail and all, in
a print from a manual of astronomy by the
French astronomer Flammarion. Opposite:
two French walking sticks with ivory knobs,
from the mid-nineteenth century, and a
Viennese light-switch, with bronze bears,
dated 1910–20.*

mid-ocean, where there are few other reference points, it
allowed them to take their bearings and keep to their
course. Long before the invention of the compass the
Phoenicians, the Vikings, the Chinese, the Greeks and the
Romans travelled the world's oceans, secure in the
knowledge that, by observing the Pole Star, they stood a
good chance of reaching their destination and eventually
returning home.

Polaris is not a star of the first magnitude. In itself it is
unremarkable and nondescript. But its value has been
inestimable. To find it is easy. It is not necessary to locate its
constellation home, the Lesser Bear, Ursa Minor, which is
neither strong nor bright. Instead simply follow a straight
line, through a fairly short tract of sky, from the last two of
the seven stars that compose another constellation – brilliant
and always visible – namely Ursa Major, the Great Bear.

There are several mythological versions of how the Bears
arrived in the sky. According to one legend, the Great Bear
was once Callisto, a nymph of extraordinary beauty, who
was loved by Zeus and gave birth to his son, Arcas, the

legendary ancestor of the Arcadians. Hera, mother of the gods, however, was jealous of the nymph and, in her wrath, transformed her into a she-bear. Callisto wandered about the world in her new guise for some years until Arcas, now grown up, met her when he was out hunting. He would have killed her had Zeus not interceded, turning mother and son into constellations and casting them into the heavens. He placed them, as the two bears, in a course around Polaris, in the center of the heavens. It was no accident. Since both constellations were situated in a zone of sky where, in northern latitudes, they never set, both mother and son would be always visible and always under divine protection.

Alternatively we can recall Callisto as the favourite nymph of Artemis, goddess of hunting, nature and wildlife. Once more, Zeus was infatuated with her and, in this story, he engineered a plan of seduction. Artemis had the frequent habit of taking on the guise of a bear and Zeus, cunning as ever, disguised himself the same to woo the nymph. The plan worked. But, when Artemis discovered what had happened, she gave full vent to her jealous fury and, in a sudden fit of anger, killed Callisto. Zeus, however, stepped in once again. He transformed his nymph into the constellation Ursa Major and, alongside her, he placed her young son, Arcas, for company.

Or maybe it was not Arcas. Another version of the story tells that Ursa Minor is actually Callisto's dog, transformed at the same time as his mistress. Arcas, in this case, should be identified with the totally different constellation of Bootes (also called Arctophylax), which lies not far from the other two. A further variation tells that it was Artemis herself, and not Zeus at all, who engineered the transformation. She changed Callisto into a bear as a preferable option to killing

her, but condemned her to wander forever through the heavens as a punishment.

It has always been hard to see how the ancients could have discerned the various images they saw in the night sky. None, however, are more difficult to see than the bears. Even with charts they are difficult to make out, blessed as both bears are, with exceedingly long tails and obscure bodies. Indeed, it is much easier to imagine the outlines of the more mundane objects that have contributed to the alternative names of the constellations – Dipper, Plough,

Wagon. Yet, for thousands of years, people have preferred to allude to them as the Great Bear and the Lesser Bear. And the mythology from elsewhere backs this up.

The etymology of the name Ursa has been much disputed. Camille Flammarion, the nineteenth-century French astronomer, maintained in his book *The Stars and the Curiosities of the Sky* that Ursa is derived from the Greek *arctos* which, in turn, derives from the Sanskrit root *ars* ("brilliant") and refers to the white fur of the polar bear. Then, too, the Arabic names of certain stars in Ursa Major

*An elegant and valuable ashtray, supported by bears, from late nineteenth-century tsarist Russia. It is made of bronze and mother-of-pearl, with four inset oval garnets. The bear is an integral part of Russian culture, tradition and folklore.*

allude to parts of the bear's anatomy. There may be a connection here, given the many cultural exchanges that have taken place over the centuries among the peoples of the Mediterranean.

More astonishing, though, is the fact that in the folklore of some Native American tribes the largest constellation also represents a bear. In the oral tradition of the Delaware Indians, there is a legend that tells of a bear (the four stars in a square) which fled through the heavens pursued by three hunters (the three stars that form the tail). The bear was

*An early twentieth-century English silver and enamel match-holder.*

*Two English hand-carved wooden candle-
holders for the table, dated 1910. Opposite:
a painted plaster Santa Claus from the
United States, dated about 1905. Among
his gifts is one of the earliest Teddy bears.*

never caught and it continued, day after day and year after
year, to run away from the hunters, describing a broad circle
in the northern skies. Perhaps this legend also sprang from
the Mediterranean and arrived from Asia in the course of
migrations across the Bering Strait, or it may just be an
extraordinary coincidence. But it is worth noting that in the
Native American legend the bear has no tail and, indeed, is
rather more easy to picture in the sky. As the constellation
revolves anticlockwise around the Pole Star it does indeed
appear to be chased by its hunters.

According to other legends, the constellation represents
the detached head of a bear followed by the rest of its body,
in a desperate attempt to catch it. One hopes it will not
succeed. If it ever does, says the legend, and the two pieces
join up together, the end of the world will be at hand.

# Hero of the tale

Once upon a time, according to a popular legend from the Chukchi peninsula, that extreme outpost of Siberia facing Alaska, the Bering Strait did not exist. Asia and America made up a single, immense continent. The geography changed the day that an enormous white bear challenged a strong and valorous Chukchi hunter to a duel. The hunter accepted the challenge and the two began to fight, extending their struggle to the strip of land that separated the Pacific and Atlantic Oceans. The battle was protracted, violent and terrible and, little by little, the two rivals scooped out with their feet the entire battle ground on which they stood. The narrow tongue of land was reduced to nothing, exposing the two seas, which then came crashing together. The story goes on to say that both man and animal tumbled into the water, to the great advantage of the bear, which found itself in its natural element, and to the considerable peril of the hunter, who risked drowning. Nevertheless the intrepid Chukchi managed to climb on to the bear's back and be towed to the shore.

     This last point is particularly interesting in the context of

*A brown bear fishing for salmon, carved in stone by a Northern Native American. Following double page: another small masterpiece, this group carved from turquoise by a Cheyenne craftsman.*

a legend that depicts the bear as such a powerful and aggressive animal, because it alludes to another side of its nature that seems helpful, honourable and respectful of its human rival. The big assumption here, of course, is that the bear was aware of the passenger he was carrying. But even if the opposite was true, and the animal was quite ignorant of having a stowaway on board, certain conclusions can be drawn. A psychologist might argue that the legend underlines the duality of the bear's character: it shows the animal as extremely strong and dangerous, yet rather dull of intellect and undoubtedly less alert and astute than humans. And, as we have already seen, such a bear does not inspire the same degree of terror.

East of the Bering Strait, on the mainland of North America, the Native Americans, too, treated bears with adoration, respect and fear. One legend tells of a rather naughty young girl who went out with her sisters to gather berries and fruit in the nearby fields. Unlike her sisters, who were merrily singing while they worked, this little girl was continually chattering, complaining and bemoaning her lot.

The local bears were evidently offended by the girl's lack of musical sense and conspired to abduct her. To gain her trust they assumed human guise and carried her back to their den. Here she was married to a male grizzly and, from this union, a pair of cubs were born, half-bear and half-human. But the girl had not been forgotten by her human family who eventually discovered her in her new home. Her brothers arrived and promptly killed her grizzly husband. Yet, before the bear died, he imparted his wisdom and magic to his wife and sons. The two bear-boys later grew up to become expert hunters and fabled teachers in the art of traps and snares. Eventually they became the chiefs of the tribe.

Possibly because of its humanoid appearance the male bear, over the centuries, has been the subject of many fabled amorous incidents involving human girls and women. There are quite a few myths and legends that mention such encounters, although they adopt contrasting viewpoints. Sometimes the bear is gentle and protective: having found a young woman lost in the forest he proceeds to feed her, rescue her, console her and take care of her until, inevitably, they fall in love. At other times things are different: the bear uses less gentlemanly tactics. Several legends of the North-West American tribes tell of women raped by bears.

There has always been a popular belief that bears have a particular fondness for pretty, solitary girls wandering through the forests. Women of the North American Tlingit tribe, for example, were well aware of this weakness, for as soon as they picked up the tracks of a bear, they would begin to shout aloud the animal's praises, at the same time begging it not to assault them. Contradictory behaviour, perhaps, especially if the bear was known to be vulnerable to female charms and understandably flattered by the compliments being paid him.

The North Americans were not alone in accusing the bear of stealing women. In European villages, young men were often troubled by the presence of bears as though they might be powerful rivals for the hearts of their loved ones. Nor was this an idea likely to have been imported from across the Atlantic for it was rife long before navigators from Europe set foot on the New World.

In China, too, the bear was traditionally seen not only as a symbol of strength and courage but also as the very image of virility. Chinese women who dream of a bear are destined to give birth to a boy, while the Kazakhs of Mongolia were in the habit of attaching a bear's claw to the

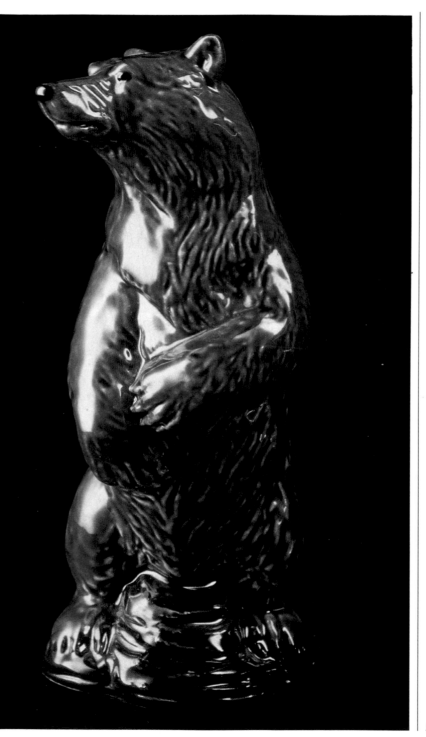

Within the illustration:
BEAR, BEAR, DON'T GO AWAY
TO COME AGAIN SOME OTHER DAY
I WILL LOVE YOU IF YOU STAY
I WILL LOVE YOU ANY WAY

SEAL

cradle of a newborn male baby, as a symbol of power and safety.

Yet, whereas popular legend in three continents make frequent mention of brutal encounters, fleeting affairs and even the occasional happy and lasting marriage between male bears and human females, there are hardly any instances of the reverse situation. She-bears do not, it seems, lust after human males and rarely can a man be induced to make romantic overtures to the bear. Nevertheless, there is one story of a young man who married two she-bears, and another of a liaison between a Menominee brave and a bear which resulted in the birth of another bear-hero. This course of events echoes, more or less, the Korean myth of the legendary hero Tan Gun.

By and large, therefore, mythology portrays the male bear as the seducer while the female bear is cast in the role of the loving, caring mother who rears and protects her cubs. And yet, in a sense, the female is always the real hero. It is she who produces the invincible, half-human, half-animal creatures and the extraordinary heroes destined to enter the realm of folklore. In the world of bear-myth, that rearing is no simple task.

The Greeks and Romans held the belief that bear cubs were always born prematurely and not fully formed, resembling indistinct pieces of flesh without head, skin or limbs. The mother would then use her tongue to lick these tiny raw individuals into life. It was thanks to her that they gradually took on their definite, perfect shape. Such accounts are to be found in the works of Aristotle, Pliny the Elder, and Ovid in *Metamorphoses*. Rabelais and Shakespeare alluded to the same habit some centuries later, and even today vestiges of the belief are to be traced in the French saying *"ours mal leche"* ("badly licked bear"), to

*Two enamelled tin bears, one a ballerina, the other a playboy. Opposite: an American postcard of the early twentieth century illustrating a somewhat precocious bear. In myths and legends of many cultures the bear has often played the role of seducer.*

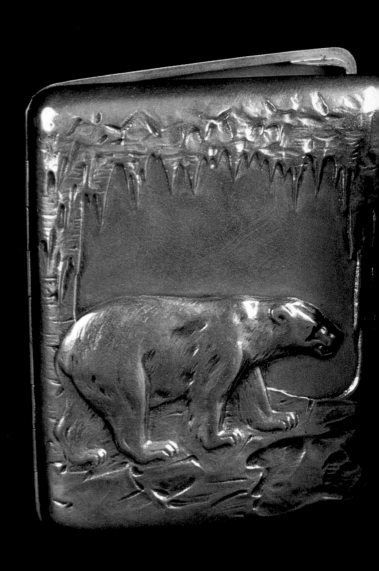

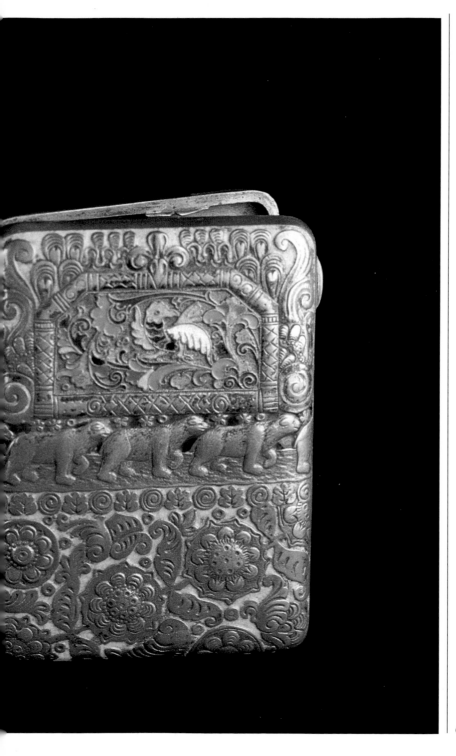

63 of page

63

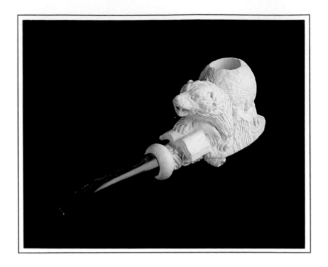

describe a raw, clumsy person, and, in our own expression,
"lick into shape."

In fact the she-bear has a profound role in almost all bear
legends, and she is generally regarded as kind. Even when
the mythical heroes are not her own sons, the mother bear is
likely to be transformed into a nurse, as in the Greek legend
of Paris, abandoned as a baby and suckled by a she-bear, or
in the Old English poem of the hero Beowulf who grows
up to slay the terrifying monster Grendel.

Milk, incidentally, is not the only food provided by the
bear that is credited with having sustaining and invigorating
properties. The growing Achilles, for example, was fed on
the bone marrow of a bear; and Nordic sagas tell of warriors
who drank the blood of the animal in order to acquire
strength and valour.

Bear legends don't necessarily, however, always contain a
human element. Frequently they tell only of the bear itself.
An Arapaho legend, for example, relates how the bear lost a

*This Chinese pottery bear is very fat, almost like a Buddha, and it also has an enormous tail, which is either a lapse on the part of the potter or a deliberate flight of fantasy. Following double page: bears ready for a repair job in a service station.*

part of its tail as a punishment for stealing. The bear's tail also features in stories from the Far North. The Locheux (and also the Chukchi, their Asiatic counterparts) tell of how the ancestral bear went out to fish and let his tail dangle in the freezing water. The ice entrapped his tail and he was unable to save it. The sins of the fathers were visited on the children and from that time on the race of bears was compelled to put up with the stump they now possess.

The bear's tail, in fact, seems to have given rise to a good deal of puzzlement and wonder over the years. More so, indeed, than any other part of the creature's anatomy, excepting its paws. Curiously, though, there has been no consensus of opinion. Stories don't agree on the appendage's length. The heavenly Great Bear and the Lesser Bear are both represented with very long tails, which has no connection with reality. In some Chinese and Japanese statuettes, too, the bear, notwithstanding zoological fact, is portrayed with a lengthy tail. On the other hand, the Iroquois maintained that the animal is completely tailless, and an ancient Chinese text, the Shanhai Jing, stated that the brown bear had an anus both above and beneath the tail. The dispute is confusing, especially when we realize that, although the bear's tail is admittedly quite short, it can be measured with reasonable accuracy.

Yet another disputed subject in mythology is where the first bear came from. A Finnish legend has no doubts as to its human links. It tells of a youth who, one fine day, decided to climb a tree. As he clambered up the branches his clothing started to get in the way and hampered his progress. So he shed one garment after another until, eventually, he was naked. But this was hardly an improvement, for the branches now scratched and tore his skin. The young man thus implored a god to deck him out

*Two more fishing bears. The one shown above, grasping a salmon in his jaws, comes from Alaska and is made of rhodonite; the one opposite is a rare Japanese clockwork bear of 1950 from the Alps company, which, thanks to its battery motor and two small magnets, catches a fish and puts it in the basket.*

with a fine coat of fur. The god obliged and the ancestor of all bears was created.

A more imaginative and poetic Nordic legend describes how the bear was born when one of the daughters of the air, out for a walk on a cloud, dropped some flocks of wool in the water. A wood nymph collected them, interwove them with threads of gold and fashioned a cradle for her baby. Whether or not it was the addition of magic wool, the fact is that the baby grew up to be strong and hairy, and was given the name Bear. Because he was also good and loving, his mother furnished him with teeth and claws, whereupon he

began to wander through the meadows and woods during
the summer and to shelter in the depths of the Earth during
the winter. This is behaviour that the bear still maintains.

The bear's link with the world of gods and celestial
powers is further reflected in other cultures. In the Chinese
bas-reliefs of tombs from various dynasties, bears are
portrayed with functions that are definitely associated with
the divine world and the passage of the soul to the beyond.
In the legend of Gun, for example, the spirit of the father of
Yu the Great, founder of the first Xia dynasty, assumes the
guise of a bear. Among the Zou of Taiwan, the supreme
god, who has the likeness of a man, is dressed in the skin of a
bear. Other very early Chinese works of art depict ritual
dances centered upon the bear, underlining once more the
sacred and totemic character of the creature. Little is known
of the ceremony except that the priest who performed the
dance was dressed in a bear skin and wore a wooden mask
with four golden eyes, and these features are remarkably
similar to those of Eskimo ritual dancers and those of many

North American tribes.

The bear cult is to be found, too, in Labrador, where legends relating to the most important deity, the god Torngarsoak, describe him as an invisible being yet with the appearance of an enormous white bear. This reflects the belief held by several populations of the American Far North that the polar bear was almost a supernatural being.

Across the Pacific again, the island of Hokkaido, most northerly of the Japanese archipelago, is the land of the Ainu. These people may be of Indo-European origin, for they have little in common with the Japanese and Mongols, and their cultural traditions are (or were until quite recently) a strange mixture of southern and typically northern elements. One of these is the cult of the bear.

The Ainu regarded the bear as the personification of the mountain god Kim-Un-Kamui, the hero of innumerable legends. Stories of his exploits, transmitted orally, through folklore, and also displayed in decorative works of art, are legion. He also provides the basis of many Ainu religious rites, perhaps the most well known of which is the so-called "sacred dispatch" of the bear.

A newly born bear cub is captured, kept in a cage close to the village and lovingly fed and reared. (It is said that at one time a local woman actually suckled the cub herself, and there are Japanese prints to illustrate the occasion.) When the cub was two or three years old, and thus still quite young, it was ready to be dispatched to its celestial ancestors.

The ceremony, which was attended by people from all the neighbouring villages, went on for several days and would climax with the strangling of the unfortunate creature. This, they believed, would liberate the cub's spirit from its flesh so that it could rise to the heaven of divine bears, its illustrious ancestors, as a messenger and ambassador of the tribe. Not, perhaps, a fate that the bear cub would

*A French postcard of the 1930s. The bear is probably a Steiff because it shows some typical hallmarks of the German factory, such as the large feet and the upturned wrists.*

D.É.DÉ
PARIS
169·1

73

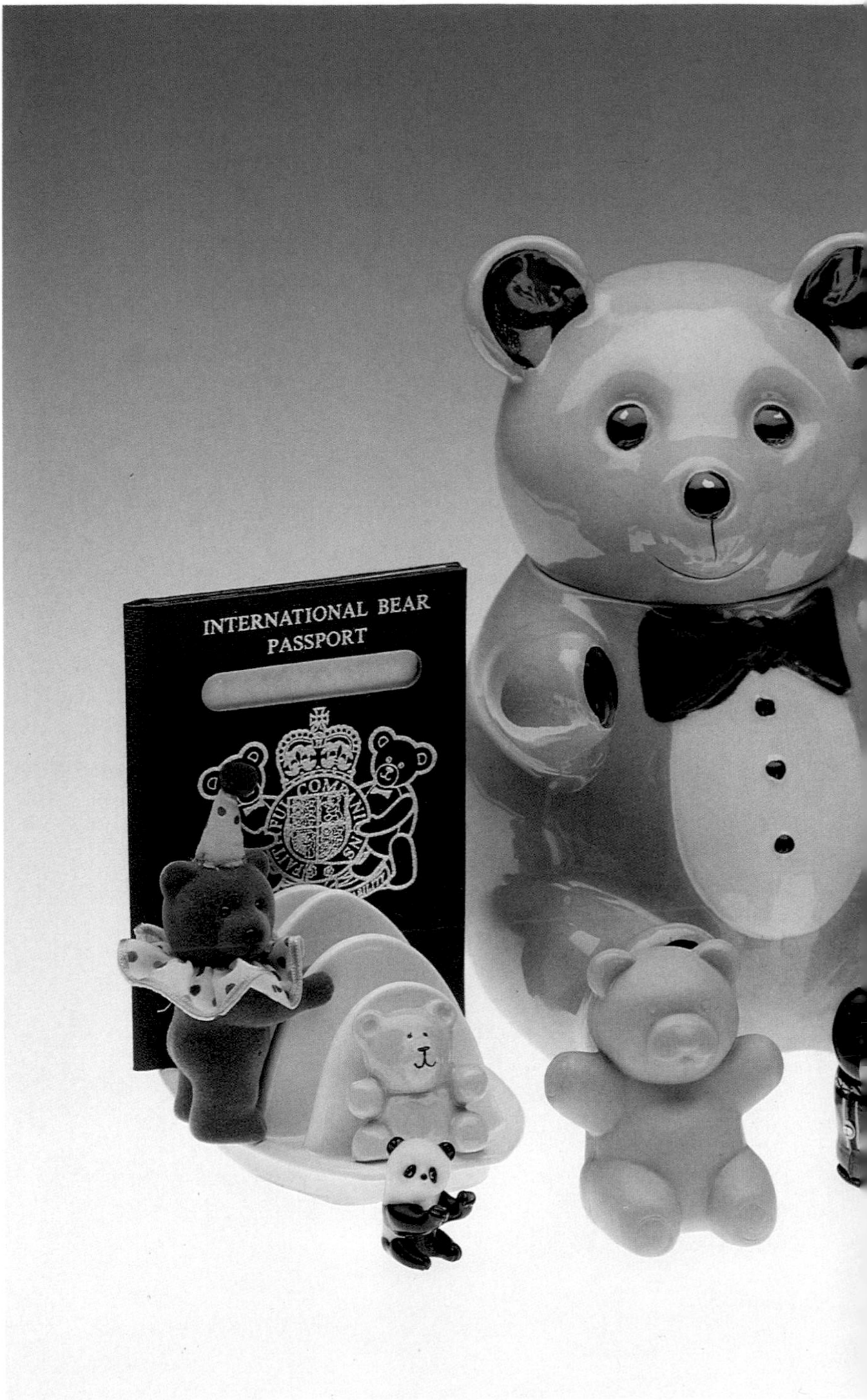
INTERNATIONAL BEAR
PASSPORT

welcome but it was not intended to be cruel or heartless. Indeed, while it may seem doubtful to us today, the Ainu were unquestionably motivated by the best of intentions.

In Europe the bear was the king of the forest, incomparably powerful, ferocious, aggressive, brave, and, by definition, a warrior. One Germanic legend speaks of a race of warrior bears who were invincible because they were motivated by a near-mystical battle frenzy. Another story tells of the lord of a castle who suddenly fell into a trance while, at the same moment, away on the battlefield, his soldiers, preparing for an enemy attack, were confronted by a huge and terrible bear. The bear turned and put the enemy army to flight, at which very moment the lord of the castle awoke, drained and exhausted, as if he had fought and defeated the foe at the head of his troops.

Since the bear is so frequently seen as a strong, courageous warrior, a hero defending his country or city, it is hardly surprising that he should often be portrayed on flags and coats-of-arms. The bear appears as an emblem throughout Europe, particularly in the regions of the Alps. He figures on the insignia of towns such as Madrid, Biella, Appenzell, St Gallen, Orsières and Andermatt, to name just a few. Most notably, however, he is the emblem of Berlin and Berne.

Even though he was once accompanied by an eagle and was occasionally depicted as quite small, in a secondary position, the bear has been the emblem of Berlin for 750 years. More latterly, of course, he has stood on his own. In fact it was in the thirteenth century, when it became necessary to distinguish the seals of the various towns in Brandenburg (which until then had been confusingly similar with their eagles and turreted walls), that Berlin formally adopted the bear.

*A fierce warrior bear guards the Kramgasse in Berne. The street leads straight to the famous Bärengraben or bearpit, the city's symbol. Preceding double page: a group photograph of Teddy bears from different parts of the world, hence the need for a passport.*

*A bronze, dated 1835, by the French animal sculptor Antoine Louis Barye, showing a bear fleeing from dogs. Opposite: more warrior bears from Berne, prepared to defend the city.*

But the link between the animal and the town literally goes back forever. The assonance between Berlin and *Bär*, German for "bear," is no coincidence. The two words may, in fact, be linked by etymology. There are those who believe that the city derived its name directly from the *Bärlein*, a "bear club." Others point to the twelfth century margrave, Albrech der Bär, so nicknamed because of his valour in battle, who is commemorated in the knightly order of Albert the Bear, founded in 1836 by his descendants, the dukes of Anhait-Dessau. Yet others go for a more banal explanation – simply that the forests around Berlin swarmed with so many bears that it was natural for them to be adopted as part of the city's symbolism. Large numbers of bears roamed all over Europe, and it would have been as natural for such animals to be portrayed in local art as for people in Africa or Asia to choose the lion or the tiger.

So closely was the bear associated with the social and political vicissitudes of the city that in 1918 it ousted the imperial eagle and emerged proudly alone, standing erect on two legs, on the Berlin coat-of-arms. Then, in 1934, the Nazi regime transformed it into a warlike beast with gaping jaws, flaming tongue and enormous claws.

After the war, when Berlin was occupied by victorious allied troops, the official emblematic bear was again a much gentler creature, with mouth closed. But this did not last long. In 1954, with Germany well on the road to economic recovery, the image of the bear reappeared on both sides of the Wall, once more sporting long claws, tongue protruding from open jaws armed with deadly teeth.

The bear that features on the coat-of-arms of the Swiss

*Above: the Berne coat-of-arms on the tympanum of one of the city's neo-classical palaces. Opposite: three bears, symbols of the city of Berlin, from the 1940s and 1950s; the tin perambulator is earlier, from around 1915.*

capital of Berne is equally fierce and aggressive, depicted walking along an oblique gold band against a red background. Here, too, theories abound. As in the case of Berlin, assonance and common etymology are mentioned, but the generally accepted explanation refers to the legend of the city's founder, Berchthold von Zähringen, who in 1191 killed a bear on the future site of Berne. Certainly a bear is depicted on the oldest coat-of-arms in the city, dating from 1224. Moreover, a Celtic-Roman statue, obviously from a much earlier period, has been found in the outskirts of Berne: it represents Artia, goddess of fertility, portrayed as a she-bear.

Today the capital of the Swiss Confederation continues to pay homage to the bear in many forms: there are statues in squares and on street corners, and there is the famous pit where, every Easter, children (at a safe distance) come to greet the newborn bear cubs. It is another reminder, perhaps, of the long-standing link between the species. The citizens of Berne, in fact, sometimes compare themselves to bears. They draw comparisons in their strength, their affability and their peaceful nature. Others, less generously, say it is because of the way the Bernese walk and because of their argumentative temperament.

# Enter Teddy bears

The magic moments that occur at intervals in the course of human history are seldom easy to recognize except with benefit of hindsight. Only then can one perhaps conclude that the time was ripe for a particular idea, discovery or invention. It is as if, suddenly, all was ready and in place for the emergence of something that was already in the air, present though as yet unexpressed, already part of the collective human unconscious, merely waiting for someone who was more aware, more capable, more sensitive than others to recognize it, grasp it and bring it to light. Such are the people who have been responsible for some of the great turning points in history, the consequences of which have been far greater and deeper than anyone could ever have expected or predicted.

These world-shaking ideas, discoveries and inventions are not necessarily unique to one individual or one place. Often they appear to be generated at the same time in the minds of several people who may be living thousands of miles apart, belonging to different cultures and in entirely different situations, so that it is virtually impossible to establish the

*This clockwork bear of 1955 from Japan, with its puffed-up cheeks and staring eyes, is blowing soap bubbles. The craftsmanship is superb. It dips the ring into the dish of soapy water, raises it to its mouth and blows through it.*

true founder or originator. Jung called this phenomenon synchronism.

Synchronism happened with the invention of the telephone, and with the motor car, the aeroplane and the light bulb. On a rather more modest level, it also happened with the Teddy bear, probably the most important children's toy to be invented in this century.

Everyone is agreed on the Teddy bear's date of birth: 1903. But as to where it was born, there are two different versions, partly based on historic documentation, partly cloaked in legend.

The first version places the Teddy bear's birthplace in Brooklyn, and attributes its invention to the intuition and entrepreneurial flair of a young émigré couple from Russia, Morris and Rose Michtom. It is a typical story of an American dream in which courage, generosity, business acumen, ambition to succeed, and money all play their share. It is worth looking at in some detail.

In November 1902 the United States President, Theodore Roosevelt, travelled south in search of a solution to the problem of the state boundaries of Louisiana and Mississippi. Between political meetings, a bear hunt was organized in his honour. The President often engaged in this form of hunting which was very fashionable at the time, requiring, as it did, some courage. This particular trip, however, went badly. The only prey was a young brown bear cub which, exhausted by the chase, stunned and bleeding from the dogs and the beaters, was captured, tied to a tree with a noose around its neck and presented to Roosevelt for shooting. The President refused to kill it, remarking: "It would be unsporting, and if I were to do it I could not look my children in the face."

The story does not go on to relate what happened to the

*The original cartoon of President Theodore Roosevelt and the bear cub, as it appeared in the Washington Post in November 1902. The drawing was the inspiration for Morris Michtom, the American father of the Teddy bear. Opposite: a small Steiff Teddy bear of 1950, which is still manufactured today in identical form.*

unfortunate bear and whether it was dispatched by a less generous hunter, whether it ended its days behind bars in a zoo, or whether it was set free. It does, however, tell that some days later the President's noble words were enshrined in his official biography thanks to a cartoon drawn by Clifford Berryman and published in the *Washington Post* on 16 November. It was a clever picture. In the background a hunter is clinging to the collar of a bear cub while in the foreground the President, with an eloquent gesture of the hand, makes it quite clear that he is unwilling to shoot the tethered animal. The caption to the drawing, which read "Drawing the line in Mississippi," had a double meaning. Not only did it allude to the boundary dispute between the two states but it also pointed to the support that Roosevelt was giving to the cause of human rights in the American Southern States.

This caricature of President Teddy (as he was familiarly known), however, gained a popularity that was far beyond its political, racial or topical connotations. So much so, in fact, that five years later it was reprinted, slightly modified, in another newspaper, the *Washington Star*. On its first appearance it had, in any case, enough impact to influence one individual at least.

That person who saw the original drawing and was much affected by it was Morris Michtom, a small shopkeeper from Brooklyn. Always on the lookout for ideas and products

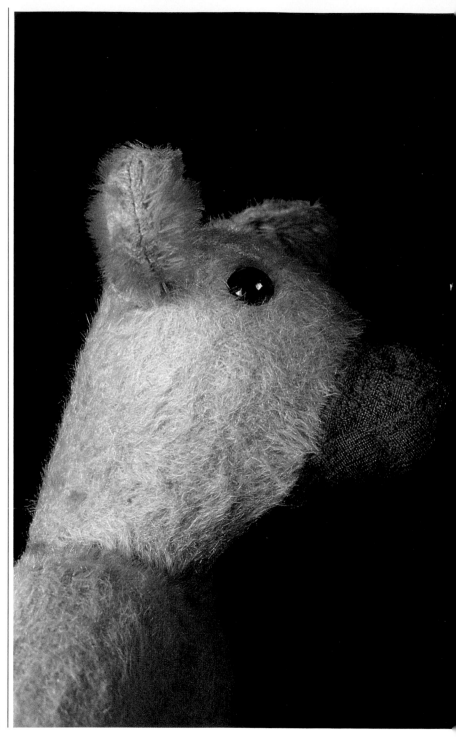

that would draw the customers (and perhaps in tribute, too, to the culture and traditions of his native land of Russia), Michtom asked his wife to make a couple of soft toy bears, and to display them in the shop window together with the cartoon from the *Washington Post*. The bears were made of brown wool, the body being stuffed with shavings, and with two black shoe buttons as eyes. They were an immediate hit, and Mrs Michtom was kept busy turning out one bear after another to keep the till ringing.

Her husband, meanwhile, discovered that he had an instinctive flair for marketing. He went straight to the top, writing to the President of the United States himself to request formally that he authorize his name being used for the toy bears. The President duly replied in the affirmative, and so the Teddy bear was born. Although the President felt some initial qualms about lending his name to advertising children's toys, his doubts proved unwarranted. As for the young Russian immigrant, his brilliant idea was triumphantly rewarded. Five years later Michtom's modest business was the foundation for the Ideal Novelty and Toy Company, even today one of the most flourishing toy manufacturing concerns in the United States.

Until 1906 the former toy shop owner was virtually the only American manufacturer of the Teddy bear, but in due course the toy animal, unprotected by patents, was copied by a large number of other manufacturers. Soon there were so many that it is now extremely difficult, if not impossible, to say exactly where a particular example of an American Teddy bear of that period originated. Michtom, nevertheless, was always credited with having invented it and, on his death in 1938, the White House sent official condolences to the family.

*Three bears for the bathroom: a bar of soap, a nailbrush and a Teddy that changes colour when it is dipped into warm water. Preceding double page: two historic specimens, the one on the left made in the United States, the one on the right a Steiff, both from the 1920s.*

This, then, is the American account of how the Teddy bear came into being. But at the very same time, on the other side of the Atlantic, in the heart of Europe, a twin to the Michtom bear was also being born.

In a village near Stuttgart, Germany, lived Margarete Steiff, a woman who had been stricken by poliomyelitis and was confined to a wheelchair. She was an expert seamstress and maker of children's clothes but she also spent much of her time making charming little fluffy toy animals. Most of them were pin cushions in the form of an elephant and, with these, she had already had some commercial success at the Leipzig Fair.

Margarete's nephew, Richard Steiff, however, suggested some other ideas. He was an amateur painter whose subjects included the bears at the Stuttgart Zoo and thought that a toy bear cub would be a delight. So his aunt duly produced one and exhibited it at the next Leipzig Fair in March 1903. The new toy was virtually ignored, but on the last day of the Fair it did attract attention. Just before closing time an

American visitor called at the Steiff stand. Hermann Berg,

*A peddler of popcorn, above, and a peanut vendor, opposite. Both are battery-driven clockwork bears, made in Japan during the 1950s and 1960s.*

the toy buyer for the New York department store George Borgfeldt & Co, saw the little bear and fell for it immediately. He ordered 3,000 samples.

Once introduced to the United States, the bear enjoyed a second stroke of luck when it was seen by the man commissioned with the decorations for the wedding dinner of President Theodore Roosevelt's daughter. At this point the story becomes rather confused; some say that a number of bears were ordered which then found pride of place at the wedding table itself, exciting the interest of the President and his guests. From there to assuming the name "Teddy" bear was but a short step.

Others, however, say that on this occasion there was not the slightest sign of a toy bear. Indeed the most important

*One of the very first rag bears made in 1903 by Margarete Steiff, the mother of the European Teddy bear. Note the long legs and the black buttons that serve as eyes. Opposite: a postcard of 1930. The bear in the wheelbarrow is also probably a Steiff.*

person at the wedding, Alice Roosevelt herself, admitted to the late Peter Bull, who owned one of the largest collections of Teddy bears, that she had a genuine dislike of bears and would never have agreed to have them, even in such harmless form, at her marriage festivities.

Whatever the truth, the Steiff factory at Giengan turned out some 12,000 Teddy bears in 1903. Within four years the total output had jumped to 974,000. From then on, the company officially devoted itself to the manufacture of toy bears and adopted the head of a bear as its trademark. Eighty years later the symbol still appears on the labels attached to the left ear of every animal made by Steiff.

But the story does not end here. Even as the United States and Europe competed for the honour of fathering the Teddy bear, a new contender entered the race: England.

In the early nineteenth century England had made a key

contribution to the world of children's toys when it introduced the wax doll. So when the Teddy bear appeared on the English market it, too, was claimed as native born. The story quickly spread that the Teddy bear's name was a diminutive of Edward, and specifically of King Edward VII, who was said to be fond of bears as testified by his visits to those animals' enclosures at London Zoo.

Independent experts in tracing the family tree of the Teddy bear are not inclined to give much credence to this theory. Still, whether the first Teddy bear spoke King's English, American English or German, there is no doubt that he and his relatives and descendants have made their indelible mark in the realm of toys and brought delight to successive generations of children everywhere.

*Opposite: these two bears are from England – the one in front a Chad Valley product of 1920, the other, of unknown make, dating from 1930. Below: a pair of German bears – the one in front is a Steiff, the other is one of the many imitations of Giengen products.*

# Hunting for bears

It has been happening since time began: hunting bears with spears, bows and arrows, arquebuses, rifles, traps and snares. Nowadays hunters even resort to helicopters, tracking their prey from the air. They call it sport.

Fortunately, some bears have at last found protection in national parks and are subjected to nothing more dangerous than tourists' cameras. But there are other ways also, and safer ones still, by which we can catch a glimpse of these majestic animals. And we do not even need to go out into the wild to do it. For there they are, tucked away in the pages of books written by authors who have clearly shared our affection for them. And we need look no further than our nearest bookshop or library to come away with our precious trophies.

Here, on the following pages, is a small cross-section of excerpts from world literature in which bears play a prominent role.

*A curious porcelain inkwell of the 1920s from France. The bear's head rotates sideways to allow the ink to be poured in. The posture of the bear is identical to that of the live bear in the photograph from Berne on page 17.*

*Opposite and on page 103: two drawings by Dino Buzzati for his book,* The Famous Bear Invasion in Sicily.

DINO BUZZATI, **The Famous Bear Invasion in Sicily**

*Once upon a time, Sicily was invaded by bears, who came down from the high mountains under the leadership of their king, whose daughter had been seized by the hunters of the plains. The fable, a symbolic mixture of surreal invention and popular ballad, is full of dramatic happenings, related with gusto by Buzzati, who also illustrates it with his drawings. After the most exciting episode, when the bears, now lords of the island, begin to succumb to human faults and vices, the story concludes happily: the bears return to their ancient mountain retreats and the tranquillity of nature. Thus ends their temporary transformation into humans.*

The characters

*King Leontes.* He is the king of the bears; the son of a king who in his turn was son to a king. He is big, strong, courageous and good (and intelligent, too, though not enormously so). . .
*Various ghosts.* They are ugly, but harmless. They are the spirits of humans and of dead bears. It is hard to distinguish one kind from another. When they transform themselves into ghosts, bears lose their fur and their snout gets shorter: so they differ little from humans, although the bear ghosts are somewhat bigger. . .

. . . "Go back to the mountains," said Leontes slowly. "Leave this city where you have found wealth but not peace of mind. Take off those ridiculous clothes. Get rid of the gold. Throw away the cannons, rifles

and other devilries that the humans have taught you. Go back to what you were before. How happy we were in those remote caves open to the winds, as you never were in those miserable palaces full of cockroaches and dust! The forest mushrooms and the wild honey still seem to us the most exquisite food. Oh, drink once more the pure water of the springs, not the wine that ruins health. You will be sad to lose so many fine things, I know, but afterwards you will feel more contented and you will also become more beautiful. We have got fat, my friends, that is true, we have grown a paunch."

. . . And next day the bears took their departure.

To the amazement of the humans (and also somewhat to their dismay, for by and large they had liked the animals), they left

the palaces and houses just as they were, without removing even a pin; they piled up in the square all the weapons, clothes, flags, uniforms, etc., and set them on fire. They distributed all the money, down to the last cent, to the poor. And in silence they filed through the street which thirty years beforehand they had marched along in victory.

RUDYARD KIPLING, **The Jungle Book**

*In the classic children's story, also made into an enchanting animated film, the hero is a small boy, Mowgli, who has been abandoned in the jungle and raised by a she-wolf. And who better than the bear, Baloo, to play the part of fatherly adviser, teacher and protector? This is how Baloo is described in the first story,* Mowgli's Brothers:

Then the only other creature who is allowed at the Pack Council – Baloo, the sleepy brown bear who teaches the wolf-cubs the Law of the Jungle: old Baloo, who can come and go where he pleases because he eats only nuts and roots and honey – rose up on his hindquarters and grunted.

"The man's cub – the man's cub?" he said. "*I* speak for the man's cub. There is no harm in a man's cub. I have no gift of words, but I speak the truth. Let him run with the Pack, and be entered with the others. I myself will teach him."

"We need yet another," said Akela. "Baloo has spoken, and he is our teacher for the young cubs. . . "

*In* Kaa's Hunting, *Baloo warns Mowgli of the Monkey-Folk:*

"Listen, Man-cub," said the Bear, and his voice rumbled like thunder on a hot night. "I have taught thee all the Law of the Jungle for all the peoples of the Jungle – except the Monkey-Folk who live in the trees. They have no Law. They are outcasts. They have no speech of their own, but use the stolen words which they overhear when they listen, and peep, and wait up above in the branches. Their way is not our way. They are without leaders. They have no remembrance. They boast and chatter and pretend that they are a great people about to do great affairs in the Jungle, but the falling of a nut turns their minds to laughter and all is forgotten. We of the Jungle have no dealings with them. We do not drink where the monkeys drink; we do not go where the monkeys go; we do not hunt where they hunt; we do not die where they die. . . ."

*Soon enough the monkeys launch an attack on Mowgli, Baloo and Bagheera, the Black Panther. They are eventually routed by Kaa, the Python. Mowgli's friends lick their wounds. Bagheera asks:*

". . . Baloo, art thou hurt?"
"I am not sure that they have not pulled me into a hundred little bearlings," said Baloo gravely, shaking one leg after the other. "Wow! I am sore. . . ."

". . . Mowgli," said Bagheera angrily, ". . . my ears and sides and paws and Baloo's neck and shoulders are bitten on *thy* account. Neither Baloo nor Bagheera will be able to hunt with pleasure for many days. . . . What says the Law of the Jungle, Baloo?"

Baloo did not wish to bring Mowgli into any more trouble, but he could not tamper with the Law, so he mumbled: "Sorrow never stays punishment. But remember, Bagheera, he is very little."

. . . Bagheera gave him half-a-dozen love-taps. . . . When it was all over Mowgli sneezed, and picked himself up without a word.

"Now," said Bagheera, "jump on my back, Little Brother, and we will go home."

One of the beauties of Jungle Law is that punishment settles all scores. There is no nagging afterwards. . . .

103

## JACK LONDON, Love of Life, in The Call of the Wild and Selected Stories

*The hero, injured, alone and lost in the region of the Great Bear Lake, that zone of Canada lying on the verge of the Arctic Circle, is struggling desperately to stay alive. After many days of walking, exhausted and weak from hunger because he has caught nothing by hunting and his ammunition has gone, he suddenly finds himself face to face with an enormous animal.*

Before him stood a horse. A horse! He could not believe his eyes. A thick mist was in them, intershot with sparkling points of light. He rubbed his eyes savagely to clear his vision, and beheld not a horse but a great brown bear. The animal was studying him with bellicose curiosity.

The man had brought his gun halfway to his shoulder before he realized. He lowered it and drew his hunting knife. . . . The bear advanced clumsily a couple of steps, reared up, and gave vent to a tentative growl. If the man ran he would run after him; but the man did not run. He was animated now with the courage of fear. He, too, growled, savagely, terribly, voicing the fear that is to life germane and that lies twisted about life's deepest roots. The bear edged away to one side, growling menacingly, himself appalled by this mysterious creature that appeared upright and unafraid. But the man did not move. He stood like a statue till the danger was past, when he yielded to a fit of trembling and sank down into the wet moss.

*Smokey Bear, highly popular in the United States, is the symbol, mascot and spokesman of the U.S. Forest Fire Prevention Campaign. He first appeared on a poster in 1944.*

WILLIAM FAULKNER, **The Bear** in **The Greatest American Short Stories**

*This is the story of a boy who grows up believing in the myth of an enormous bear and the ritual of hunting it. The animal is not evil, just very big, and it has taken on a real personality, being named Old Ben.*

The old bear had earned a name, through which ran not even a mortal animal but an anachronism, indomitable and invincible, out of an old dead time, a phantom, epitome and apotheosis of the old wild life . . . . : the old bear solitary, indomitable and alone, widowered, childless, and absolved of mortality.

*In time, the wild and primitive environment known as the "wilderness" comes to dominate the boy's life, and the bear itself becomes a kind of parent figure. When, finally, the two meet, the young hunter does not shoot, because, unconsciously, he sees in his antagonist . . .*

. . . an old bear, fierce and ruthless, not merely just to stay alive, but with the fierce pride of liberty and freedom, proud enough of that liberty and freedom to see it threatened without fear or even alarm; nay, who at times even seemed deliberately to put that freedom and liberty in jeopardy in order to savour them, to remind his old strong bones and flesh to keep supple and quick to defend and preserve them.

*Left: this 1920s drawing by E. H. Shepard is of Winnie-the-Pooh reaching for honey. Opposite: another lover of honey is this pottery moneybox bear, also from England, made around 1970.*

WILLIAM SHAKESPEARE, **The Winter's Tale**

*This is one of Shakespeare's last plays, a story of friendship, jealousy, death and revival. Leontes, king of Sicily, unjustly suspects his wife, Hermione, of being unfaithful to him and orders Antigonus, a lord at his court, to dispose of Hermione's newborn daughter, Perdita. After a voyage to the distant land of Bohemia, in what Shakespeare describes as a "desert country near the sea," Antigonus reluctantly leaves the baby to die. As he lays her down tenderly, he hears a terrible noise:*

> Farewell!
> The day frowns more and more: thou'rt
> like to have
> A lullaby too rough: I never saw
> The heavens so dim, by day. A savage
> clamour!
> Well may I get aboard! This is the chase:

I am gone for ever.

Antigonus is indeed doomed. His soliloquy ends with what is possibly the most famous of Shakespeare's stage instructions: [*Exit, pursued by a bear*].

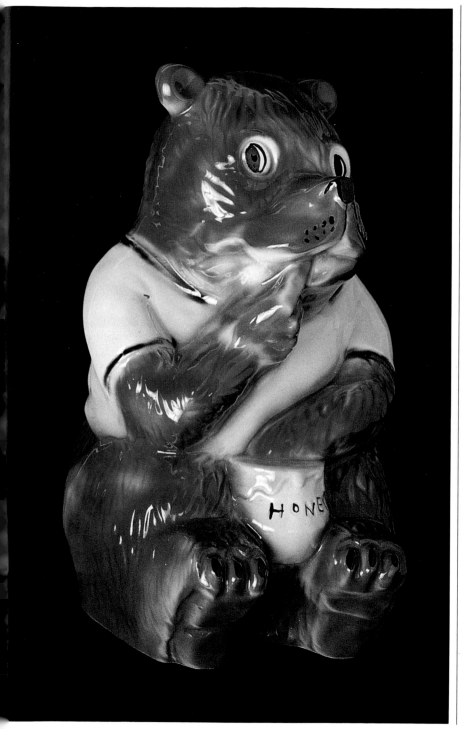

A. A. MILNE, **Winnie-the-Pooh**

*This book, with its sequel, is a perennial children's favourite. Its central characters are Christopher Robin, son of the author, and his toy bear companion, Winnie-the-Pooh. Here Winnie-the-Pooh finds himself in an embarrassing situation: in his attempts to reach some honey, of which he is enormously fond, Pooh approaches the bees by floating up with a balloon. But the bees are angry at the trick, so Christopher, in order to prevent his friend getting hurt, shoots the balloon. The little bear descends gently to earth.*

But his arms were so stiff from holding on to the string of the balloon all that time that they stayed up straight in the air for more than a week, and whenever a fly came and settled on his nose he had to blow it off. And I think – but am not sure – that *that* is why he was always called Pooh.

*Below: a complimentary ticket for an Italian film made by Orso (Bear) Production. Opposite: another drawing by E. H. Shepard of Winnie-the-Pooh, with Christopher Robin.*

LA ORSO PRODUCTION

presenta

LA MERAVIGLIOSA FAVOLA DI BIANCANEVE

BIGLIETTO OMAGGIO
VALIDO PER 4 PERSONE fino esaurimento posti

# Household words the world over
**Brief glossary of bears in four languages**

### English

**bear** *n.* (from Old English *bera*, related to Scandinavian *bjorn* and Germanic *bero*) carnivorous or omnivorous mammal of the family Ursidae ‖ (*Stock Exchange*) one who sells short, expecting a fall in prices ‖ (*astronomy*) either of two constellations in northern hemisphere, i.e. Great Bear, Lesser Bear ‖ (*fig.*) a clumsy or coarse person ‖ *like a bear garden*, a scene or place of noise and confusion ‖ *be a bear for something*, show a special aptitude, resolve or enthusiasm ‖ *be a bear with a sore head*, be in a bad mood ‖ (*Stock Exchange*) *bear the market*, speculate in stocks with a view to lowering prices.

**bearish** *adj.* bearlike, rough, surly, rude ‖ (*Stock Exchange*) unfavourable, tending to cause a fall in price.

**bearskin** *n.* tall, black, fur hat worn by soldiers of Guards regiments.

### French

**ours** *n.m.* (from Latin *ursus*) bear ‖ (*fig.*) *ours, vieil ours*, rude, coarse or unsociable person ‖ *ours mal léché* (*literally*

Opposite: Winnie-the-Pooh climbs a tree, on the lookout, as always, for honey. Below: Pooh again, this time more passive and looking slightly perplexed. Left: the bear and the bull breathless after the crash of Wall Street and other stock markets around the world in October 1987. This cartoon by Sergio Manni appeared in the Italian weekly Milano Finanza.

badly licked bear), boor, lout, ruffian ‖ *vendre le peau de l'ours,* selling something before having it, counting one's chickens before they are hatched ‖ *le pavé de l'ours (from a fable by La Fontaine),* doing harm with the best of intentions, thus wishing to be saved from one's friends ‖ *se balancer, se dandiner, tourner comme un ours en cage,* prowl about like a caged animal.
**ourson** *n.m.* fur hat formerly worn by grenadiers.
**Nounours** *n.m.* (*child's language*) Teddy bear.

## Italian

**orso** *n.m.* (from Latin *ursus*) bear ‖ (*fig.*) rude, coarse or unsociable person ‖ *ballare come un orso,* dance clumsily ‖ *vendere la pelle d'orso prima che sia morto,* selling something before having it, counting one's chickens before they

are hatched ‖ (*Stock Exchange*) orso in Borsa, tendency of prices to fall.
**orsaggine** *n.f.* surly, gruff, boorish person.

## German

**Bär** *n.m.* (from Germanic *bero*) bear ‖ (*fig.*) quarrelsome person ‖ *jemanden einen Bären aufbinden,* give someone a drink ‖ *wie ein Bär schnarchen,* snore loudly ‖ *man soll nicht das Fell des Bären verkaufen, bevor man den Bären hat,* selling something before having it, counting one's chickens before they are hatched.
**Bärendienst** *n.m.* poor service.
**Bärengesundheit** *n.m.* good health, bless you (after sneeze).
**Bärenhaüter** *n.m.* lazy person, loafer.
**Bärenhunger** *n.m.* ravenous hunger.
**Bärenkälte** *n.f.* intense cold.
**Bärenkraft** *n.f.* enormous strength.
**Bärenruhe** *n.f.* calmness, imperturbability.
**Bärenruhig** *adj.* calm, tranquil.
**Bärenstimme** *n.f.* loud voice.
**bärig** *adj.* (Bavarian *dialect*) exceptional, very beautiful.

## Acknowledgements

This book would not have been possible without the contributions of many collectors and bear lovers. The author would like to extend particular thanks to: Paolo Beccaris (Turin), Mirella Cannata (Milan), Madeleine Deny (Si tu veux, Paris), psychologist Alessandro Fonti (Milan), psychoanalyst and bear lover Sergio Levi (Turin), astronomer Enrico Miotto (Milan), psychoanalyst Maria Grazia Spinoglio (Milan), Eugenio Zucco (La Giostra, Turin), Francesca Pinchera (Milan), Danilo Mainardi (Modena) and the Pollock Museum, London.

The publisher thanks Gruppo Mantero.

Pages 14 and 15: 1940 toy kitchen from Ingap of Padua.

The extract from *The Bear* by William Faulkner is reproduced by kind permission of Random House.

The extract from *Winnie the Pooh* by A. A. Milne is reproduced by kind permission of Dutton Children's Books.

## Picture sources

The bears and the objects photographed in this book belong to the following collectors:
Giorgio Coppin (pages 4, 28, 33, 43, 60, 61, 68–9, 74–5 and 91)
Sergio Levi (page 25)
Guido Orsi (pages 8, 12, 23, 26–7, 38, 39, 45, 47, 48, 49, 53, 54, 56–7, 59, 62–3, 64, 66, 70, 78 and 98)
Eugenio Zucco (jacket), pages 7, 9, 11, 14–15, 16, 19, 21, 24, 31, 34–5, 36, 40, 41, 50, 51, 65, 71, 73, 80, 83, 84, 87, 88–9, 92, 93, 94, 95, 96, 97, 107 and 109)
All the photographs are by the author in collaboration with Anna Giorgetti. Those on pages 33, 43 and 74–5 are by Marco Melloni.